The Game Changer in Your Marriage

Kalu Igwe Kalu

The Game Changer in Your marriage

Copyright: © 2016 Kalu Igwe Kalu
Tel: +2348023572650
Email: passionintensified@gmail.com

All rights reserved. No part of this book may be reproduced or transmitted in any form or by any means, electronic or mechanical, including photocopying, recording, or by any information storage and retrieval system, without permission in writing from the author.

Published by Global Reach Publishing LLC 2015

ISBN: 9785049647
ISBN-13: 978-9785049640

Printed in the United States of America

To God Be the Glory,

Great Things He has done.

DEDICATION

I dedicate this book to My Rock in marriage who gave me a wonderful wife and three great sons.

ACKNOWLEDGMENTS

Every beautiful marriage out there is an inspiration and a motivation to me.

Don't make the mistake to think that yours is not beautiful. Your Marriage can be the most beautiful in the world. You just have not seen it.

Please, take a look again.

CONTENTS

	What This is All About	Pg #1
1	God's Plan is Not Ambiguous	Pg #3
2	Always Have this in Mind	Pg #5
3	Don't Remove Your Miracle from God's Plan	Pg #6
4	Put Your Best Foot Forward in Your Marriage	Pg #8
5	Be Bold, Never Be Afraid	Pg #10
6	Say Good-Bye to Loneliness	Pg #12
7	Become Matured	Pg #14
8	Make Every Experience Count	Pg #16
9	Fight the Battles of Marriage	Pg #19
10	Change Your Habits	Pg #22
11	Love Does Not Go on Holiday in Marriage	Pg #24
12	What Makes Marriage Easy	Pg #28
13	When Surprises Come	Pg #29
14	I Will Do My Spouse Good All Through this Year	Pg #32
15	What a Victorious Marriage Will Do for You	Pg #33
	About the Author	Pg #35
	About the Book	Pg #36

WHAT THIS IS ALL ABOUT

This is a great year. A wonderful year to grow and thrive in your marriage. A year to make mistakes and grow. A year to become matured and excel. It's also a year to learn and be victorious.

Marriage Is Beautiful Inc. has taken it upon them to study the times as regards marriage, to know the areas that the devil is hitting marriages hard and to make effort to always be one step ahead of the adversary of our marriage.

Every couple has to be on top of their game and put their best foot forward always so that their marital life can be enjoyed and they will live in harmony peace and contentment.

What we see these days are marriages where the couples are silently divorced. They live in the same house as neighbours but not as husband and wife. Most times, the only thing that holds them together is the kids. Nobody wants to jump ship due to what family, friends and the church will say.

This report will help take care of this problem. It will help couples to become focused as they enter the year. They will know what to expect and what to do at each point in time to be their best in their marital activities.

It is my prayer and earnest desire that this manual will be of help and give you the keys to unlock all that you have ever hoped for in your marriage.

Enjoy as you read!

GOD'S PLAN IS NOT AMBIGUOUS

God doesn't make mistakes. When He designed your marriage, He also created a plan for your marriage. Gods design for you and your spouse this year is for you to have a glorious marriage that is successful, prosperous, healthy and fruitful. Anything short of this glorious life in your marriage this year is not acceptable, reject it. It's not God's plan for your life and your marriage. God's plan is clear; yes it is; it's not ambiguous but rather simple, He makes all things beautiful and fruitful.

www.beautifulmarriages.com

"God doesn't make mistakes. When He designed **marriage**, He also created a plan for your **marriage**."

Kalu Igwe Kalu

ALWAYS HAVE THIS IN MIND

Always Always remember this, a beautiful marriage is not a union without problems or challenges but a coming together of two different people who will have challenges from time to time but have made up their mind to continue to love one another.

This year, no matter what happens in between, don't give the enemy, the devil the chance to infiltrate and cause disharmony in your marriage. Disharmony is the only thing the enemy can use against Gods plan for your marriage this year. Seek oneness with your spouse this year. Seek to be in agreement and have oneness of purpose and direction.

DON'T REMOVE YOUR MIRACLE FROM GOD'S PLAN

Many a times, we willingly or ignorantly remove ourselves from Gods plan by our actions and inactions.

It is one thing that God has a plan for your marriage and it's another thing to willingly tap and flow into Gods plan. There will be spoilers this year, factors and situations trying to torpedo the plans of God for your marriage and if possible to make you become a victim.

A victim of divorce, separation and unhappiness. These spoilers come hidden in our daily experiences and encounter with our spouses.

They come hidden in that snide remark your spouse will make, they come hidden in that unintentional and intentional mistakes your spouse will make. Whatever it is, no matter the situation you have to make up your mind that you will maintain a positive and appreciative attitude at all times this year so that the unity and oneness of your family will not be compromised.

PUT YOUR BEST FOOT FORWARD IN YOUR MARRIAGE

Like I said earlier, Gods plan for your marriage this year involves prosperity, protection and increase. With this knowledge, I will like you to willingly put your best foot forward and tap into this agenda.

In your prayers as a couple, always pray for increase, protection and prosperity. As you make your business plans, think big because whatever you agree together as a couple God will make it to come to pass.

This also goes to our finance and all that we hold dear to us. Believe for growth in your business, seek to invest and do business with boldness because God has got your back this year.

It is better you advance from where you are now and make effort as a couple to go to higher grounds. God is on your side.

www.beautifulmarriages.com

"When you keep studying your **spouse**, your **spouse** will never outgrow you."

Kalu Igwe Kalu

BE BOLD,
NEVER BE AFRAID

In this year, a lot of us are going to grow in the work of our hands. God is going to take many of us to great heights that we have never imagined.

Many of us will receive double promotions and uncountable increase in our finances. My advice is this; as your spouse grows, grow with them. Grow into the capacity God is taking them to. We have to grow with our spouse.

We have to grow with their career, their emotions and their successes in life. Don't be left behind in their past grief's and failures. Mature and grow with your spouse. One way to do this is to keep studying your spouse always.

As you grow, if you study your spouse and find out that they are not growing with you, take it easy and pull them along or they will drag you back. Our marriage this year is upward and forward only.

Moving back is not allowed. So, keep studying your

spouse and as you do that your spouse will never outgrow you.

SAY GOOD-BYE
TO LONELINESS

This is a year you will say good bye to loneliness while being married. It is a year where you will get the fullness of all your spouse has to offer. You see, most couple who feel lonely in their marriage is so because they have taken a stand without their spouse.

There is nothing more comforting and assuring than knowing that where you stand, your spouse is also standing there with you. Knowing that where you go, even if your spouse cannot go there with you that he or she is supporting you.

You are about to take a major step in your life and career this year, right? There is this major life changing decision you must make this year; am I correct? Will you say that your spouse understands why you are about making such a decision? Please, as you go now to communicate your heart to your spouse, just bear this in mind; you too are on the same side working together towards a glorious future.

BECOME MATURED

As we move into the year, I would like you to understand that the problems you have had in times past in your marriage actually came to strengthen your marriage.

Always ask yourself, what have I learnt from this? With this mindset, you will actually come to see problems that will arise between you and your spouse as an opportunity to strengthen and build your marriage.

Only let yourself to be cool headed through it all while asking God to give you the grace to deal with all that comes against your marriage with maturity, faith, wisdom, excellence, dignity and integrity.

www.beautifulmarriages.com

> "The memories we share in **marriage** is a constant inspiration and hope that our **marriage** will keep getting better and better."
>
> Kalu Igwe Kalu

MAKE EVERY EXPERIENCE COUNT

It's quite easy for anyone to lose sight of the fact that, it's our day to day experience over time, both the good and the bad that adds up to the memories we share in marriage.

Take a look at your relationship with your spouse, let's say three years ago. Was there a time you had an experience that was so fierce that you nearly broke up with your spouse or you felt like giving up? If that same experience were to happen again now, would you still react the same way you did three years ago.

Why? I may ask. If your answer is no, it's probably your relationship is getting more and more matured. If you are honest with yourself, you will admit that the nasty experience you had three or more years ago actually helped in strengthening your marriage and getting you more matured in your marriage.

My advice and encouragement for you this year? Make the most of every situation you're presently dealing with now and seek to turn it into a memory that you will love to remember or a story you will love to tell your children, let's say, three years or more from now. Never give up on your marriage.

www.beautifulmarriages.com

"Sometimes, having a beautiful **marriage** can mean that you will have to stand and fight for what is rightfully yours."

Kalu Igwe Kalu

FIGHT THE BATTLES OF MARRIAGE

It's quite easy for anyone to lose sight of the fact that, it's our day to day experience over time, both the good and the bad that adds up to the memories we share in marriage.

Marriage is not a child's play. In-between the love, romance and softness of marriage, Marriage is also where battles are fought and won. Couples must stand together this year against forces that will come to steal and kill all that they love and cherish. The devil is after your marriage, but don't worry God has already given you the victory.

You have to stand and fight for your wife. You have to stand and fight for your husband. Don't let no devil steal your wife or husband from you this year. Don't run at the slightest scent of pressure and trouble. Stand and fight those negative forces of lust and waywardness in your spouse.

Refuse to give them permit in your spouse. Your spouse is not their dwelling place. Don't let anybody shut down your marriage for you. Your spouse deserves your prayers. Pray for them like you never done before. Your marriage must succeeded. *Marriage is Beautiful!*

www.beautifulmarriages.com

> "**Marriage** is not a child's play. In-between the love, romance and softness of **marriage**, **marriage** is also where battles are fought and won. You have to stand and fight for your **marriage**."
>
> — Kalu Igwe Kalu

CHANGE YOUR HABITS

We all have so many habits, many, we picked up along the way before we got married. Now that you are married, there is one habit you need to keep and practice all the days of your life.

The habit that always prompts you to forgive and be kind to your spouse, all the days of your life, without looking back.

The best way to change a habit is to pick up a new and better one. Drop the habit of nagging and raising dust in your marriage at every little thing, pick up a new one like appreciating every little thing your spouse does for you.

You could even decide to change the tone you use in speaking to your spouse this year. Learn to speak softly to the love of your life, speak that they may understand your heart and see the love inside.

These little things will build up to that big testimony you will give later on in the year.

LOVE DOES NOT GO ON HOLIDAY IN MARRIAGE

The countdown of families who will give their testimonies of how they triumphed in their marriages later on this year starts now. So, remember, love does not go on Holiday in marriage.

Make up your mind that as we move on into the year, that you will fall in love with your spouse all over again. Always be kind to your spouse, forgive when you are wronged, it will be your game changer this year.

If you are finding it difficult to be kind to your spouse Just remember what it takes to be nice and kind as a human being first and extend same to your spouse.

When you are a kind man or woman, it will become very easy for you to show kindness to your spouse. As a wife be kind and as a husband be kind to your wife also. Husbands find it difficult to resist a kind and loyal wife.

www.beautifulmarriages.com

> "**Husbands** find it hard to resist a kind and grateful **wife**."
>
> Kalu Igwe Kalu

For those husbands who find it hard to display soft emotions towards their spouse, I already know that Showing emotions is not a natural attribute for men but any husband who has a big appetite of pleasing his wife can learn how to.

Forgiveness and Kindness is a formula that transcends geography, religion and race. With this combination working together in your marriage, there is hardly any marital storm a couple cannot ride. The storms will come with much intensity that you will think the marriage will not survive but when these two factors of forgiveness and kindness are allowed to play itself out, the marriage will always bounce back and flourish much better than it was before the storm. This formula does not say it will be smooth all through but it guarantees you a happy ending.

WHAT MAKES MARRIAGE EASY

The countdown of families who will give their testimonies of how they triumphed in their marriages later on this year starts now. So, remember, love does not go on Holiday in marriage.

God's grace is more than enough to carry you through this year, always come back to Him when there is a problem in your marriage. God can see you through any difficulty you may have. You need God in your marriage. As for me, the rock I go to whenever I have challenges in my marriage is Jesus. All you have to do is pray and invite him into your marriage. Jesus makes marriage easy. He will calm any storm in your marriage. Don't run from pillar to post looking for help where there is no help. Jesus is all your marriage needs. Give Him a try in this day and age.

WHEN SURPRISES COME

The countdown of families who will give their testimonies of how they triumphed in their marriages later on this year starts now. So, remember, love does not go on Holiday in marriage.

There will definitely be surprises for everyone who is engaged in the business of marriage this year. Your concern is going to be how to turn every surprise to beautiful. The devil has demons who are at his beck and call 24 hours to do only one thing, to cause as much confusion as possible in your marriage. Specialists who have been assigned to make sure that married couples will keep seeing situations that will overwhelm them and make them do things that will defile and dishonor them. That is why every marriage must be vigilant and strong in prayer this year. This is a year of victories. Victory that you did not get for yourself but victory given to you by God. Demons or no demon, your marriage is impenetrable because God has got your back. God himself will fight for you.

All you have to do is to keep going back over and over again to Jehovah Marriage, the one who makes marriages beautiful, the giver of joy and the he that dwells in constant light. When situations will arise that will want to knock you down, just fall back on Him. Even if you have already fallen, just fall back on Him again. Your marriage will sing the victors' song this year.

The Game Changer in Your Marriage

www.beautifulmarriages.com

"I will never **cheat** on my **spouse**."

Kalu Igwe Kalu

I WILL DO MY SPOUSE GOOD
ALL THROUGH THIS YEAR

Make a commitment within yourself that this year; you will do all within your power to do good to your spouse. Let it be an ambition within you.

See it as a goal. No matter what happens, your spouse's interest is your major concern. You will see to it that they are happy as long as it is with your power to guarantee it.

WHAT A VICTORIOUS MARRIAGE WILL DO FOR YOU

When your marriage succeeds you have succeeded. Our marriage succeeding is synonymous to us succeeding in our personal lives. Failure in marriage is always seen as a failure in other things.

It demoralizes us and makes us to lose heart. Marriage has a way of setting the course of your life and putting you in a frame of mind to think of higher things and to be more prosperous than you have ever been.

This is your year. Your year of a successful marriage. There has never been a year like this for you in your married life. You shall give testimonies of the wonderful things that will happen in your life this year. Don't be afraid just match on; it shall be well with you.

This book has been written with your victory in mind. Feel free to share this book with your friends after reading. I know that the words in this book are not just ordinary words but words that has been equipped and packed with power to influence marriages positively. Forward to your friends, sisters, brothers and anyone you know who is married.

While we continue to work hard in our organization to build. Sustain and strengthen marriages, we are determined to keep producing and distributing free resources that anyone can use to tackle pressing issues in their marriage. All those who do not have the opportunity of attending our seminars can also partake in the teachings at these seminars through the free resources we make available on our website.

ABOUT THE AUTHOR

Kalu Igwe Kalu is a World Renowned Marriage Mender, Relationship Expert, Marriage Counsellor and Bestselling Author of several life-changing and impact-making books including *Marriage is Beautiful*, a book that unveils the raving beauty of marriage to all and sundry.

He is the host of first-class and success-filled *Marriage is Beautiful Couples' Banquet* and *Marriage is Beautiful Couples' Retreat* which takes place in Nigeria, USA, UAE etc. He is also the President & CEO of *Marriage is Beautiful Foundation*, an organization that has impacted millions of individuals and families online and real time through their seminars, conferences and Marriage is Beautiful Online Platforms. He speaks favor and victory daily to over 8 million online followers and call out their seeds of greatness.

He is married to *Monique Chika Kalu* and blessed with three lovely Children.

ABOUT THE BOOK

Marriage is Beautiful and you can enjoy a beautiful marriage. It does not matter what you were told about marriage or what you have known marriage to be, this is your time to seek and live your blissful matrimony to the fullest.

In this exceptionally life-giving masterpiece, *Kalu Igwe Kalu* gives you the inspiration, determination, enthusiasm, ability and skills you need to stop blaming yourself or your spouse and change your game to achieve a beautiful marital relationship.

The dedication, responsibility, education, attitude and motivation you really need are wrapped up in this package of extraordinary marital excellence.

You can really live a beautiful married life and lead a charmed life in your matrimony home. Take charge and change your marital game in this day and age so that you can make a name for yourself in your marriage and be a name to conjure with who happily makes the world a better place.

YOU CAN GET UNLIMITED MARRIAGE RESOURCES at www.beautifulmarriages.com

www.ingramcontent.com/pod-product-compliance
Lightning Source LLC
Chambersburg PA
CBHW070042070426
42449CB00012BA/3140